Branding Hacks for Successful Digital Marketing

A beginner's step-by-step guide

with AI Tutorial

and an Extensive List of Online Tools & Resources

Dawnette Blackwood-Rhoomes

Branding Hacks for Successful Digital Marketing
A beginner's step-by-step guide
with AI Tutorial and an Extensive List of Tools & Resources
by Dawnette Blackwood-Rhoomes

Branding Hacks for Successful Digital Marketing

CONTENTS

Introduction

INTRODUCTION

This textbook is a practical step-by-step guide to brand marketing online and has a resourceful collection of companies, platforms, and tools you can use. I am Dawnette Blackwood-Rhoomes, Brand Coach for several online businesses, as well as a Marketing Director for a non-profit providing educational services.

So, you have an idea for a product or service you would like to introduce to the public, but you don't know where to start. Building a brand helps you clearly decide on your product, service, target market, marketing strategies, etc.

Learning Outcomes
1. Learn the key elements to build your brand.
2. Understand your brand's mission, purpose, and goals by building your brand's persona.
3. Understand your target market and how to effectively reach it by establishing your brand's typical consumer persona.
4. Learn about your brand's logo design and how you want it to be visualized by your target market.
5. Establish your brand on social media platforms via digital marketing.
6. And finally, let's not forget about offline marketing which is very effective in the physical tangible space of your business.

How to use the guide and resources:

1. Each chapter includes the reading for the week to provide valuable information for your assignments.
2. Each chapter includes the resource guide to assist in the setting up of your brand and the assignments.
3. Each chapter includes active links to these resources. For example, use the websites Xtensio to build the persona for your consumer, and Survey Monkey to conduct your Qualitative or Quantitative research.

Welcome and enjoy the course!

Dawnette Blackwood-Rhoomes

ACKNOWLEDGMENTS

To all the young entrepreneurs and small business owners,
I wish you success in your business ventures.

CHAPTER 1

WHAT IS BRANDING?

Branding is the face of your business. It represents the DNA, the persona and core of the business. Sounds like a person, doesn't it? That's because businesses and customers are really people who we can relate to; so, we must show their personalities (personas).

We must first begin with the company. Brand Persona embodies the core belief and story of your brand. In defining the brand's DNA, you must brainstorm about what the brand is about- what words can you associate with the brand? If you could describe your brand in words and expressions, what one word would explain it or what color(s) would be associated with it? This process of carving a particular impression in the minds of consumers is known as Brand Identity. This is conveyed through colors and descriptive words, and fonts and sizes; all can convey your brand message. Also, if you were to describe it as a person, what would be the core message that would reach others? What's its essence? What's its core? In other words, what's the ethos (philosophy) of the brand?

Apple is a good brand guideline – that is, the brand represents the company well. The brand is in keeping with the company's beliefs, objectives, and mission. Of course, every good brand will also follow the company's guidelines and legal specifications. So therefore, the brand should not embrace a belief that's outside the company's values. As a result, Apple's objective to provide faster technology into the hands of the everyday consumer is its ethos or philosophy. Its brand resonates with this philosophy. Developing the Brand Persona can help the company stand out from the competition and be able to create a niche that meets the needs of the target market.

To be able to meet the needs of the market, the company must first know its market. While it's creating its own persona branding, it must also research and develop the Consumer Persona of its target market. Qualitative and Quantitative research can provide these answers and give valuable insights to your customers' needs. Use Survey Monkey (see Resource Tools) to conduct your Qualitative or Quantitative research.

Bear in mind though, that the typical consumer is complex, as are all human beings. Therefore, most companies create an Empathy Map to expand on personas for the in-house brand developers to understand the consumer better. This is done by brainstorming in-house, and so the target market is not involved. This is a process of making assumptions based on your qualitative and quantitative findings and these assumptions will paint a more vivid picture about how your customers THINK and FEEL. We will cover these variables more later.

The point to branding is standing out among your competitors as well as in the customer's mind. To begin successful branding, companies must take the time to get to know and do the research of the persona of their intended target market. If you don't understand your customer, then your branding and marketing may be vain.

Exercise

1. The first thing to do in deciding the product or service you'll offer is to determine the needs people have and how you can help to meet these needs. Note, at this point you may have an idea of what you want to offer, but it's still important to do the research to determine if there's even a demand for your idea. Maybe you'll notice that there is a greater need elsewhere that you can fill.

2. Determining the need helps you to also identify the target market. Put together a group of questions that would satisfy your need to know more about your target market – done usually by a Questionnaire or Survey. Note, both the Quantitative and Qualitative Surveys are helpful at this stage.

3. Let's pretend we've noticed a need for more organic snacks for consumers who want to snack healthily. We would need to know more about these consumers to determine whether the venture would be feasible and profitable. I've included a sample of both kinds of surveys used to gather this kind of information. Please be aware that the questions should be direct, to gain truthful data.

Qualitative research is based on opinions and experiences, and is a conversation type of research, which takes longer to conduct. It's more interactive (two-sided) and can even be done over the phone and more pointed questions can be asked.

Quantitative research is based on numbers. It's more objective and generally has a broader reach. It is a shorter study.

4. Create an Empathy Map & Consumer Profile that describes the consumer's persona from your findings in the research.

Tools & Resources:

SurveyMonkey – surveymonkey.com allows you to formulate your questions or use existing ones on the site.

Our Example

We must first determine if we have a viable audience or target market for our product or service, and if so, is there a need for it. Also, whether your brand will be able to meet this need.

To begin, we have an idea for healthy snacks, but we must first determine who will want our product. So, we will conduct a Qualitative survey, as this kind of research will yield in-depth information about our potential consumers. Please note that the sample size is small (3 people) for the purpose of the exercise. Your sample size would be much larger, of course.

We chose three professionals in various professions, as we believe our product will appeal to those working long hours who will engage in healthy snacking between breakfast and lunch or lunch and dinner. The following are the results of the Qualitative research done on healthy snacking.

Qualitative Research on Healthy Snacking

Questions	Interview # 1 Responses	Interview # 2 Responses	Interview # 3 Responses
1. Gender / Age	Male, 27	Female, 35	Female, 29
2. Occupation	English Teacher	Attorney-at-Law	Medical Resident
3. Describe your typical snacks on an average day:	Chocolates, protein bars, fruits, nut mix	yoghurt, fruit juice	ice cream and cake from the hospital cafeteria and usually after lunch or dinner, depending on shift.
4. Do you snack on the job/at school and what is your typical snacking time?	Sometimes I like to snack between classes through-out the day	Yes. At about 12 noon	Yes on my job, sometimes between rounds. I bring my own snacks - Snickers, M&Ms.
5. Do you face any barriers to healthy snacking? If yes, what are they?	Yes, healthy snacks can be expensive	Yes, sometimes there are no healthy snacks nearby; sometimes friends give you unhealthy snacks	They are pricey and sometimes the taste is not appealing.
6. If there was anything to change about your snacking habits, what would it be?	I really want to opt in for more healthy snacks	I would snack far less. I would consume less bread and biscuits	I wouldn't snack as much. I fill up on snacks and miss lunch sometimes.
7. If there was one thing you could change about your favorite snack, what would it be?	I wish there were more less sugary snacks. Every snack I enjoy, contains high levels of sweeteners	I would have less sweet in my snacks	It wouldn't be as sweet, maybe. I like pastries.
8. Do you read the labels and ingredients on snacks packages? If so, why?	Yes I do because I'm conscious about what ingredients I intake	Yes, I do. I want to see how much carbohydrates, sugars, and sodium I am consuming	I read the labels but if I really want to try something someone told me about, then I don't read the labels, haha.
9. Do you think the labeling influences your snacking purchase? If so, why?	Yes, if it's not clearly labelled I'll not purchase	Yes, If it is too much carbohydrates, sugars and sodium I do not purchase the item	Yes it influences my purchase most of the time because I want to eat healthy.
10. How likely are you to buy your favorite snacks online?	I bought snacks online when I lived in the UK and Australia. Now in Japan snacks I like are limited.	Quite likely, especially if shipping is free or cheap	Sometimes but you have to buy enough for it to be worth your while, for the shipping cost.

The results are not provided for the Quantitative research, as we utilized the Qualitative method instead. Notice questions 4 to 10 are on a rating scale and multiple-choice questions (see below). These are a bit limiting because the answers are already included and therefore the consumer is constrained from expressing his/her true feelings. As a result, if you're looking for more detailed and pointed answers to ascertain preferences, likes and dislikes, and to determine pain-points (the consumer's frustrations), then the Qualitative research approach is best.

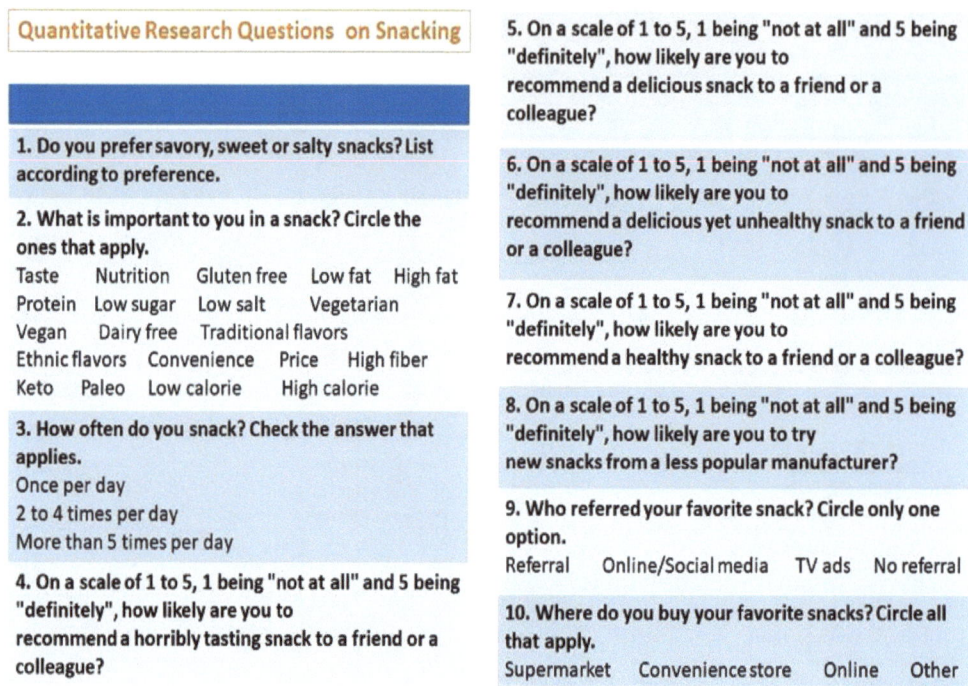

Now that we have ascertained much information about the kind of consumer our product will appeal to, this of course is the perfect segway into creating the Empathy Map (sketching out the consumer persona).

The Empathy Map

The Empathy Map is used to expand on the consumer's persona – that is, what you think the typical consumer for your brand is like. This is done in-house and by brainstorming, so the target market is not involved. However, the information collected from the research will help the in-house team make close assumptions about the consumer.

The Empathy Map highlights how your customers THINK and FEEL by considering their PAINS (what they struggle with) and their GAINS (what they value or what brings pleasure to their lives). It's about attitudes and behaviors, how they are inspired and who they are influenced by.

Lack of confidence, for example, is a pain; while wants or needs like the need to feel more confident, is considered a gain. The Empathy Map sketches what the consumer's typical day looks like (think and feel), what he/she struggles with (pains) and what he/she values the most (gains). Therefore, the in-house team put themselves in the shoes of the consumer to empathize by speculating.

We created an Empathy Map from the findings of our research. We've decided on the typical female consumer for our brand, and we named her Janice. Based on the findings of our research, she's a professional with the major PAIN POINT to become healthier.

The Empathy Map enclosed in this exercise details Janice's pre-occupations (what she's thinking/feeling), her typical environment and behavior, her influences, gains (successes in her life) and her pain-points (frustrations and struggles).

Bear in mind you are guessing what the typical consumer is like based on the findings of your research. Also, remember your product or service will not be able to solve every problem for your consumer, but it should at least resolve one pain-point.

Preoccupation (Thinking/Feeling)
Most consumers tend to be preoccupied with 3 main factors:
1. Health - Many consumers are increasingly concerned about their health and well-being, and that of their families.
2. Finances - Most people are preoccupied with ensuring their finances can meet their needs and wants.

3. Sustainability and Ethics - Consumers across the globe are becoming more conscious of their environmental impact and footprint, so they look for products and services that align with sustainability.

Most preoccupation will fall within these three categories. Our consumer, Janice, is preoccupied with health and sustainability. As a result, she is also influenced by healthy and sustainable brands.

Environment (Seeing)

In this case, consumers are most affected by their environment. Therefore, consumers who spend a lot of time on social media sites are usually heavily impacted by what they see and hear. This visual information plays a crucial role in shaping perceptions, emotions, and the decision-making process. Therefore, our consumer Janice would be influenced by her peers and social media following, and her decision-making process would be heavily impacted by trends.

Consumers are often influenced by what they see others using or endorsing - this includes brands and products.

Behavior (Saying/Doing)

What we are influenced by is also reflected in our behavior. Companies, influencers, and our peers often showcase products and experiences on various platforms. This helps to not only shape the consumer's perception but also the consumer's behavior. Therefore, decisions are usually based on how we feel about something.

Janice is influenced by an active healthy lifestyle; therefore, she goes to the gym often. This behavior (working out at the gym) is as a result of her values and the impact of other health-seekers within her environment. Note, environment can be physical as well as online. Therefore, if Janice joins a Health chat group online, that's considered an online environment.

Influence (Hearing)

We are also influenced by the things we hear or what we often listen to. Janice frequently listens to TED talks about sustainability, and is thereby influenced by such talks, podcasts, etc.

Pain (Fears, Frustration, Obstacles)

Pain-points in the consumer's life highlight their struggles and frustrations. That is, needs and wants that are not being met. For Janice, her overall pain-point is the struggle to become healthier, and it can be more specific as in not finding more healthy snacks. At this point, the consumer is looking for a way to solve the problem, so it will no longer be a pain-point, but a gain.

Here are some examples of consumers' pain-points:
1. Time Constraints - not enough time to spend doing the things they enjoy.
2. Household Chores - daily tasks can be time-consuming and tiresome.
3. Financial Stress - many people struggle to manage their expenses, and they have problems budgeting which leads to stress and anxiety over money.
4. Health and Well-being - people worry that their busy lifestyle or lack of finances will impact their health, and so a proper work-life balance is the desired goal. But if a work-life balance can't be achieved, then this becomes a pain-point.

Gain (Wants, Needs, Success Measures)

Gains in a consumer's life are typically achievements and/or successes. Here are some of the main examples:
1. Improved Health and Well-being - ensuring a healthy lifestyle. Most people consider this an achievement.
2. Personal Growth and Learning - most people want to keep learning to not only improve their economic well-being but also as a goal on their success chart.

3. Social Connection and Networking – it's considered a good thing to have friends and be able to connect with like-minded people. In some societies, having friends suggests the individual is a sociable being.
4. Having Financial Savings and Investment - many people believe in setting money aside for a "rainy-day" or for retirement. In some societies, you're deemed smart and successful to have worked and saved for retirement.

In this section, the consumer's gains are measured by his/her success in meeting his/her needs and wants.

Empathy Map

Thinking/Feeling (preoccupations)
- Personal growth (want to be more healthy)
- Professional growth (seeking a promotion)
- Wants to start own family but work focused

Seeing (environment)
- Spends a lot of time working online
- Well connected socially; meet friends in chat room
- Enjoys a closely-knit family (parents and siblings)

Saying/Doing (behavior)
- "No pain, no gain" – Ambitious, driven, motivated
- Analytical – organized and detailed-oriented
- Exercise/Gym (an overweight teenager – but focus now on BMI & Weight goals)

Age: 27 / Sex: F
Family: Single
Income: $42-$56K
New York, NY

Hearing (influence)
- Blogs about healthy foods and a sustainable lifestyle
- Avid follower of Greenpeace
- Listens to TED Talks on sustainable ecosystems and zero plastics
- Parents concerned about her single life

Pain (fears, frustration, obstacles)
- Challenge avoiding sweet pastries and unhealthy snacks. Family (parents) owns a bakery.
- Conflicted between family and professional goals

Gain (wants, needs, success measures)
- Ease in finding more healthy snacks that are reasonably priced
- Wants a good work/life balance

Write the details of your potential customer's Empathy Map. Include your consumer's preoccupations, environment, behavior, influences, pain points (fears, frustrations, obstacles) and gains (wants, needs, success measures).

Don't forget to include demographics, such as age, family status, income, and location.

_____

_____

_____

_____

_____

_____

_____

_____

_____

_____

_____

_____

_____

_____

_____

_____

_____

_____

_____

_____

_____

The Consumer Persona Profile

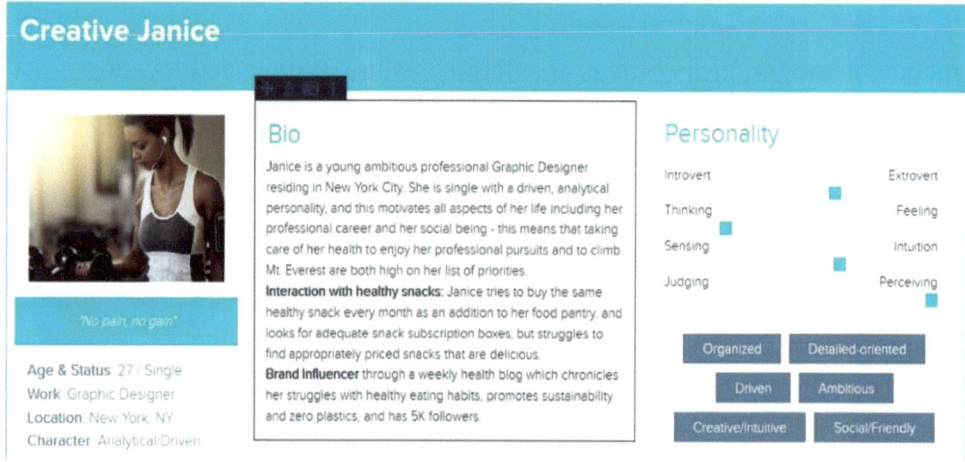

Creating the Persona Profile really brings your assumed consumer to life. It's really putting meat on the bones of what you've created so far. The more you're able to write the persona of the customer, the better able you are to understand the target market.

In our Persona Profile of Janice, she is creative, driven, hardworking and wishes to be healthier. Developing the persona can help the company stand out from the competition and be able to create a niche that meets the persona's needs. Here we notice that Janice likes organic and sustainable products – already highlighting a special need that's for a niche market. Also, pay attention to the wording that describes the types of personas such as analytical, driven, visionary, etc. This is important because by storytelling about the persona, it can tap into goals and needs to show the emotional side of the persona. You can use the persona at different stages of your business model, growth, and development.

Important Note: The Brands and the Influencers section mentioned in your Consumer Persona will give an indication of who your competitors are. These are brands which your consumer loves and they are of great influence. Therefore, our consumer Janice is a huge fan of sustainable brands such as Green Peace as noted in the Empathy Map (she wants to lead a more sustainable lifestyle).

Tools & Resources
Empathy Map: Use PowerPoint
Persona Profile and Development: Xtensio.com (extensive resource)

CHAPTER 2

DECIDE ON PERSONAL OR COMPANY BRANDING

Deciding on your style of branding will be determined by your product or service. For years my customers knew DB-R Designs, my company brand, and I was comfortable with that. However, in personal growth, as I acquired other skills and interests, with the help of my business coach, I realized that not all my skills and passions are going to fit under a company brand. In this regard, Personal Branding is highly recommended.

Once you've decided on your branding, then choose a brand name – it is recommended that you choose something that resonates with what you or your company is all about.

Exercise
1. Choose a brand name.
2. Double check the brand name's availability on namevine.com
3. Register your business online at Legal Zoom or at your local County Office.
4. Purchase a domain name for your brand on web hosting services such as Bluehost.com, GoDaddy.com, etc.
5. Find a home for your online business among the many retail hosting sites that are available such as Wix, Shopify, etc.

In the previous chapter we used organic snacks as the product we wish to highlight for this exercise. We have chosen company branding as the suitable style of branding; and the name Deber Collection of Yum for our business. At the time of writing this book, the name is available as a dot com and for several social media sites also. **Always double check if the brand name is taken or available because Namevine is not always accurate.**

Tools & Resources
Registry for dot com name availability: Namevine.com
Web hosting: Bluehost.com, GoDaddy.com
Retail hosting: Wix.com, Shopify.com, Mailchimp.com
Business Registration online: LegalZoom.com

CHAPTER 3
THE EXERCISE YOU MUST DO FIRST

D eber Collection of Yum is a conversation starter, with many people wondering about the name. Simply put, the snacks are curated from many suppliers – a collection of yummy!
Once we've determined its availability on namevine.com, it's good to secure the brand name across various social media platforms. The name should be consistent on all the sites.

For example, your Facebook name and Instagram name would carry the same handle (name) at the end:

Facebook: facebook.com/brandname
Instagram: @brandnameinstagram.com/brandname @brandname
Pinterest: www.pinterest.com/brandname
Pinterest Handle: @brandname
Twitter: https://twitter.com/brandname
Twitter Handle: @brandname

It should be noted that on Facebook, a separate page should be created for this. Other social sites can be used also, such as Pinterest and Twitter and Instagram to launch your brand.

For more creative brands and food brands, Instagram and Pinterest are powerful tools as they are great for creating and broadcasting photo stories and videos.

Tools & Resources
Facebook
Twitter
Instagram
Pinterest

CHAPTER 4
SAY IT WITH LOGO DESIGN, BRAND DNA
& POSITIONING

Your Purpose is really "Your Why"; your mission statement. If it's a business brand, then it explains the company's reason and intent for business. If it's a personal brand, then it explains your goal or purpose. The mission statement is unique and specific. It can be as long as a short paragraph, or as short as a sentence!

Including a mini version of your mission statement with your logo is called *Tagline*, and it is not only important, but also very effective. Online, the average screen time most company brands receive in consumer time is about 20 seconds before being swiped away for the next attraction. Therefore, the logo and tagline are equally important because they are the window into the soul of your brand. As a result, stick to one logo, one mission statement, one brand image - consistency. Consistency is a key component of branding, which is why consumers can easily spot the McDonald's arches or Nike's swish, anywhere.

The following is a logo design for the Deber Collection of Yum which we shortened as Yum Collection. **However, the registered name of the business would be Deber Collection of Yum.**

A nice website to design your logo is Canva and to get a little fancier with your design using animation you should consider Render Forest.

The following is the first exercise in building your brand.

Exercise
1. Design your logo and a tagline, if necessary.
2. Build a Brand DNA for your brand.
3. Create a Brand Positioning Canvas for your brand.

Tools & Resources
Logo Design & Video Maker: Canva.com, Renderforest.com
Mission + Goals: Hubspot.com
Please see Additional Logo Resources – What makes a good logo:
- Canva Logos (2023): https://www.canva.com/learn/what-makes-a-good-logo/
- Looka (2023): https://looka.com/blog/logo-redesigns-2023/
- BrandCrowd(2022): https://www.brandcrowd.com/blog/logo-design-trends-2023/

The Brand DNA Pyramid

Note that as your brand has its own logo, it should also have its own voice to educate the market about the key qualities and benefits the brand offers. This reveals the brand's DNA (structure) and it's Positioning to the target market.

Brand's Voice for Deber Collection of Yum

Brand Idea – Deber Collection of Yum provides healthy snacks and indulgence foods and beverage sourced from a variety of manufacturers and sold via e-commerce retail.

Brand/Product Persona – brand characteristics – Trustworthy and reliable (deliver on brand promise – healthy, tasty and accessible). Consumer-friendly (easy stream-lined process from purchase to delivery).

Key Qualities & Benefits

Emotional Benefits – The end goal is taste appeal which leads to consumer satisfaction and retention.

Functional Benefits – Efficiency. That is, consumers' favorite snacking indulgences can be purchased in one place with the click of a button and delivered to their doorsteps within 2-3 days (US domestic purchases).

Features & Attributes – Our products appeal to consumers' attitudes (what they believe) and behaviors (buying trends). Therefore, many people value natural, gluten-free and organic foods that are delicious. As a result, our major features and attributes are "healthy" and "tasty".

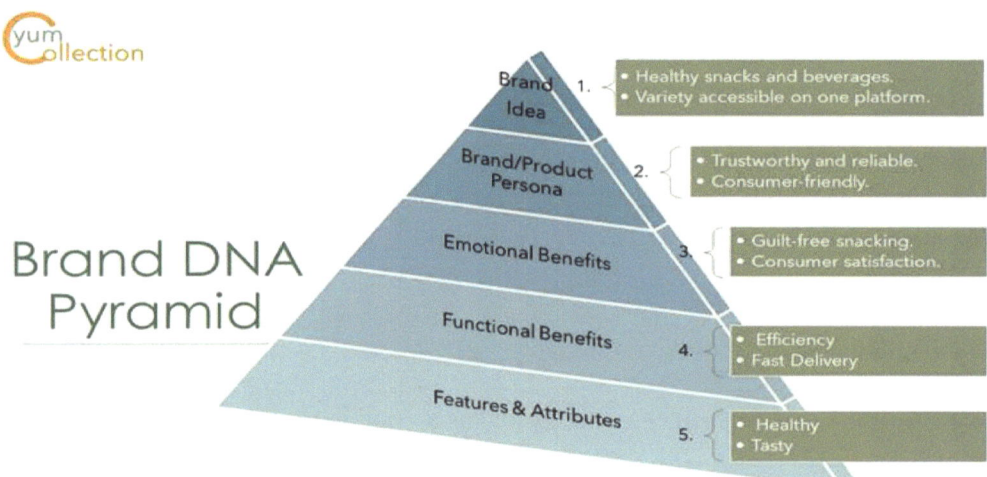

Provide the details of your Brand DNA, beginning with the brand idea, then adding the brand/product persona, emotional and functional benefits, and finally the features and attributes of your brand.

Don't forget to give your brand personality!

_____

_____

_____

_____

_____

_____

_____

_____

_____

_____

_____

_____

_____

_____

_____

_____

_____

_____

_____

Brand Positioning Canvas

The Brand Positioning Canvas covers both **the consumer** and **the brand.** It summarizes the type of consumer the brand will target, and it also summarizes the outlook of the brand – that is, how the brand will be positioned in the marketplace against its competitors. This includes a SWOT Analysis (Strengths, Weaknesses, Opportunities and Threats) of our company and product.

The Consumer

The Brand Positioning Canvas helps the company to determine how it will position its brand in the minds of the consumers. Therefore, the parameters must be set, and it begins by deciding on the target market. Deber Collection of Yum follows the Indulgence Consumer Trend, in which snacks and other indulgence foods like ice cream and chocolate bars are the major focus of snack companies.

The target market can be wide but Deber Collection of Yum's focus is to provide healthy snack choices therefore narrowing its target market to men and women 20 to 35 years who are trendsetters and key agents of change in major industries including the Snacking and Impulse Food industry.

This is the summary of Deber Collection of Yum's typical consumer (target market) persona:

Name: Janice Williams
Age: 20-35
Education: Bachelor's & Master's Degree
Occupation: Graphic Designer
Income: $42,000 - $56,000 USD/year
Family: Single
Location: New York, USA
Character: Driven/Analytical
Social grade: Middle/upper class
Goals: Become Director of Advertising in her company and climb Mt. Everest, at least once.
Frustrations: GMO foods, fast foods, plastics
Favorite Pass-time: Working out at the Gym or with a personal trainer.
Preferred Online Channels: Social media - Twitter and Facebook. These social media channels are most effective in reaching this customer through digital marketing.
Interaction with our products: Purchase the same snacks and brews every month as an addition to food pantry.

Janice is a young ambitious professional Graphic Designer residing in New York City. She is single with a driven, analytical personality, and this motivates all aspects of her life including her professional career and her social being.

This means taking care of her health to enjoy her professional pursuit and to climb Mt. Everest are both high on her priority list.

Remember, making a detailed profile of your typical target market will help your company to become more equipped to meeting customers' needs.

Brand Positioning Canvas

Target Market

DeBeR Collection of Yum follows the Indulgence Consumer Trend, in which snacks and other indulgence foods like ice cream and chocolate bars are the major focus of snack companies.

The target market can be wide but DeBeR Collection of YUM focus is to provide healthy snack choices therefore narrowing its target market to men and women 20 to 35years who are trendsetters and key agents of change in major industries including the Snacking and Impulse Food industry.

Summary of Product User Biography:

Janice is a young ambitious professional Graphic Designer residing in New York City. She is single with a driven, analytical personality, and this motivates all aspects of her life including her professional career and her social being - this means that taking care of her health to enjoy her professional pursuit and to climb Mt. Everest are both high on her list of priorities.

Example of our typical consumer (target market) persona:

Name: Janice Williams
Age: 20-35
Education: Bachelor's & Masters Degree
Occupation: Graphic Designer
Income: $42,000 - $56,000 USD/year
Family: Single
Location: New York, USA
Character: Driven/Analytical
Social grade: Middle/upper class
Goals: Become Director of Advertising in her company and climb Mt. Everest, at least once.
Frustrations: GMO foods, fast foods, plastics
Favorite Pass-time: Working out at the Gym or with a personal trainer
Preferred Online Channels: Social media - Twitter and Facebook. These social media channels are most effective in reaching this customer through digital marketing
Interaction with our products: Purchase the same snacks and brews every month as an addition to food pantry.

Problem & Solution

One major problem consumers face in this target market group is accessibility to great tasting healthy snacks, and enjoying a wider variety. By sourcing through tasting and evaluating, the company not only brings accessibility to its customers, it also brings authenticity.

Market Landscape & Advantage

The market for snacks got even wider and more evident with the arrival of Covid-19 and the need to quarantine. As a result there is a higher demand for healthy but savory snacks.

Major Snack Competitors: General Mills, ConAgra Foods, ITC Limited, and The Kelloggs Company

Niche Market & Its Competitors: Snack varieties offered snacks from various manufacturers under one umbrella, resulting in online retail competitors such as Amazon and Walmart.

SWOT Analysis:

Strengths:
•Provides healthier snacking options for customers
•Authenticity and reliability in the company's product sourcing
•Online retailing and accessible care packages that can be delivered world-wide

Weaknesses:
•The company needs a more solid marketing strategy.
•More effective execution of marketing plans.

Opportunities:
•Future opportunity to offer monthly subscription boxes of a variety of snacks, teas and brews. This niche is under-represented
•Covid-19 provides an opportunity to build customer awareness and expand market share
•Possible future sourcing of foreign snack imports into the US market

Threats:
•Although not necessarily providing healthy snacks, there are other online retailers who offer subscription boxes with a significant market share in this niche. Major online subscription retailers are KIND Snacks, SnackSack, My Keto Snack Box and Mexicrate.

Reason to Believe

Customers have confidence in our company's selections because we diligently source our offers by tasting and researching the various options, thereby bringing authenticity to the table - so to speak.

Brand Positioning Statement

For health conscious people (ages 20-35) who have difficulty finding healthy but savory and delicious snacks, we provide nutritious snacks sourced from a variety of manufacturers with ease of access via online retail. Different from our competitors our company's advantage is accessibility and variety under one umbrella.

The Brand
Problem & Solution

One major problem the consumer has in this target market group is accessibility to great tasting healthy snacks and enjoying a wider variety. By sourcing through tasting and evaluating, the company not only brings accessibility to its customers, but it also brings authenticity and variety.

Market Landscape & Advantage

The market for snacks got even wider and more evident with the arrival of Covid-19 and the need to quarantine. As a result, there is a higher demand for healthy but savory snacks. The major snack competitors are General Mills, ConAgra Foods, ITC Limited, and the Kellogg Company.

Getty Images, 2018.

However, Deber Collection of Yum can operate in a niche market by offering organic snack varieties from various manufacturers, all under one umbrella (its online retail store).

SWOT Analysis

Creating a SWOT Analysis helps the brand to determine exactly how it's positioned against its competitors. Look at the SWOT we have created for Deber Collection of Yum (below).

NOTE: The Strengths and the Weaknesses can be managed internally, which means your company has control over these issues. However, the Opportunities and Threats are external, and your company will have little or no control over these issues.

Strengths:

Considering strengths of a brand are under the control of the company, most companies aim to excel in the following areas:

1. **Recognition and Awareness:** Strong brands aim to be visible and easily recognized to be remembered by customers. They do this by having a strong logo, strong social media presence and a great product or service.
2. **Customer Loyalty:** Every company wants to retain their customers - this is known as customer loyalty. A brand with a loyal customer base has the edge over its competitors. To do this, companies ensure their product or service has value and quality, and customer service is top-notch.
3. **Emotional Connection:** Successful brands create an emotional connection with their customers. They do this by aligning the brand's value with the customer's values. How do

brands know the consumers' values? By conducting Qualitative Research and surveys to better understand their target market.

4. **Consistency:** A consistent brand shows the consumer that it's credible, reliable and trustworthy.

5. **Innovation:** Having a new innovation keeps your brand ahead of the competition. This is a strength that puts your brand in the consumer's mind as a 'trendsetter'.

6. **Wide Market Reach:** Brands with strong market presence regionally, nationwide, or globally, have a wider reach and a larger customer base. To do this, brands must market effectively and employ some or all of the above points.

Weaknesses:

As with strengths, companies have control over the weak areas within their company. Here are a few examples of where most companies usually fall short.

1. **Lack of Differentiation:** This means your brand has failed to distinguish itself from its competitors. The brand doesn't stand out to consumers. One way to resolve this is to choose an area in which the company excels and make it better.

2. **Inconsistent Messaging:** Inconsistent communication and messaging not only confuse customers but also dilute the brand's identity as trustworthy and reliable.

3. **Poor Customer Service:** This is the quickest way to lose your customer base. Negative customer experiences, lack of customer support, or slow response in addressing questions and problems leave a sour taste for your consumer.

4. **Low Product Quality:** If your service or product quality is subpar, this can destroy your brand's credibility and value.

5. **Negative Public Perception:** Make sure your brand is not associated with unethical practices, controversies, or negative news. This can lead to loss of trust and customer loyalty.

6. **Weak Online Presence:** It's necessary to have a strong online presence and lots of visibility. Otherwise, it becomes more challenging for a brand to connect with customers and reach a wider audience.

All is not lost if you detect weaknesses in your brand. Paying attention and addressing these weaknesses will only strengthen your brand in the long run.

Opportunities:

Opportunities in the market for your company are of course customizable to your brand. Therefore, companies should always be on the lookout to identify areas in which they can increase growth and use leverages to their advantage. Here are a few likely possible opportunities most brands might consider:

1. **Emerging Technologies:** Because of today's expansive growth in the field of technology, brands look for every way they can capitalize on emerging technologies such as artificial intelligence, blockchain, or virtual reality to enhance their products, services, customer shopping experience, and even marketing.

2. **E-commerce Growth:** More and more brick-and-mortar companies are getting online and expanding their reach via e-commerce retail. This allows brands to expand their online presence, reach new customers they wouldn't have had (especially those outside their region), and offer convenient shopping experiences.

3. **Digital Marketing:** Of course, with e-commerce growth comes digital marketing. Using the various digital marketing channels, such as social media, influencer partnerships, and content marketing, brands can now connect more effectively with their target market and create a larger customer base.
4. **New Distribution Channels:** Almost every company look for new and alternative distribution channels. This just refers to a different method of selling their product such as pop-up shops, kiosks, or online marketplaces.
5. **Niche Markets:** It's an amazing opportunity to identify and carve for yourself a slice of a niche market. Niche markets are areas of the market that are underserved and therefore the competition in niche markets is low.
6. **Rising Consumer Awareness:** Brands that educate their consumer often, create value and awareness. This can be done via blogging about the brand's product benefits and value. Companies should not miss out on this opportunity. It creates customer engagement and retention.

Taking advantage of these opportunities, put most brands ahead of their competitors, and help companies to stay attuned to industry trends within the industry.

Threats:

External threats like competition, economic downturn, supply chain disruptions and regulatory changes are all beyond a company's control, and brands should have a game plan to combat these. Here are some potential threats that brands should be aware of:
1. **Competition:** This is a given. Competition can be a game-changer and can mean the death of a company. Therefore, brands should always plan to be one step ahead of their competitors by looking within (using their strengths) to increase market share and profitability.
2. **Market Saturation:** If your company is part of an oversaturated market with similar products or services, then it will be difficult for your brand to differentiate itself. In this scenario, getting customer retention and capturing new customers will be a struggle.
3. **Change in Consumer Preferences:** Trends come and go, and this means consumer preferences will change along with the trends. Losing the appeal of customers is a scenario no company wants to contend with.
4. **Economic Downturn:** Recessions or downturns in a market happen when the economic tide changes in a country. This can lead to a reduction in customer-spending both on and offline, impacting profitability and growth.
5. **Supply Chain Disruptions:** If your suppliers and manufacturers are on strike or if there are any other disruptions such as natural disasters, civil war or unrest, outbreaks or pandemics, then this affects production and delivery of your products, which in turn affect sales, profitability and in the end, customer retention.
6. **Regulatory Changes:** Countries are known to make changes to regulations and compliance requirements, and this will affect how your brand does business. Companies must always keep updated on current regulatory changes to prevent legal issues.

Companies must take a proactive approach to threats with continuous monitoring of market conditions. To help overcome threats, brands must be flexible and adaptable.

These are just a few examples in which a brand can excel. Remember, growth into a strong brand takes time, effort, and consistency. Every brand is unique.

List the details of your brand's SWOT, highlighting the most critical strengths, weaknesses, opportunities, and threats to the success of the brand.

Think about how these factors will affect or impact your target market.

_____

_____

_____

_____

_____

_____

_____

_____

_____

_____

_____

_____

_____

_____

_____

_____

_____

Now that we have a more solid understanding of the core beliefs of the company (Brand DNA) and who its primary consumers are (Consumer Persona), we should keep the following points in mind:

Points to Remember

1. Curate the suppliers.
2. Decide whether your company will be dropshipping (where the manufacturing company mails the product to your customer after purchase) or warehousing (where you stock your products and wait for consumers to buy before shipping). In most cases, companies have their own private labeling and usually choose warehousing in this instance. For Deber Collection of Yum, because several suppliers are involved, dropshipping would be ideal to cut down on stocking cost. Please note however, that not all manufacturers and suppliers offer dropshipping services.
3. Prepare the social media sites you've chosen by uploading the company's logo to the sites.
4. Blog. Making daily posts about topics around your product or service is really a good way to enter a market even before you've begun selling. This introduces the company to the market and consumers become familiar with what you're all about (Brand Positioning).

Congratulations! You've now ready for the next step: marketing!

Tools & Resources

Brand Pyramid & Positioning Template: edrawsoft.com, and/or PowerPoint
Images: Gettyimages.com

CHAPTER 5
WHAT IS BRAND MARKETING?

You have identified your product and your target market; but how do you even begin to market your brand to the customers? The answer: Brand Marketing. The key to Marketing is to know your 4Ps of marketing.

➤ Product (what will you offer)
➤ Price (what is your best price that will cover your costs and yield a profit margin)
➤ Place (where will you be selling to your customers)
➤ Promotion (depending on your target market, how will you promote your product or service).

In knowing these fundamentals of marketing for your product or service, you can now begin thinking about the ideal way to market the brand overall. Marketing your brand entails further steps.

It is said that the typical attention span for the average consumer is 8-20 seconds. Therefore, as a brand marketer you want to choose your words and visuals wisely. This is why brand marketing is not only the act of marketing a brand. It also involves various processes that lead to branding – that is, having a knowledge of your brand's 4Ps, as well as employing creative variables (logo, branding, customer persona, etc.).

At this point, marketing the brand becomes easier, and you're ready for the next step which is to create the storyline and visual advertising.

Storyboards are often used in advertising. To create familiarity and relatability, many advertisers start with a catchy quote to create the story through words or music. Can a brand grow? Strong brands leave room for growth- so they don't talk about products or services but instead the stories of brands encapsulate an experience or a why (why they do what they do).

STORYTELLING TECHNIQUES
1. The Pixar Model (pitch/format) – "once upon a time, every day...but one day... because of that... until finally" – this technique tells a story from start to finish using these words to link each scene. Commonly used in Disney Pixar movies (hence the name). This technique proves to be relatable with consumers.
2. The Hero's Journey Model - the mighty warrior and the never-ending fight against evil, witches and wizards, the dragon and the supernatural. "The hero is tested and must use his experience (initiation) to gain a new world order (return)" (Wikipedia, 2023). This is according to Joseph Campbell's *The Hero's Journey- the hero of a thousand faces* – the approach for his hero's adventure. This storytelling technique has been adopted in advertising, and the customer (the hero) faces his problem and wins when his problem is resolved.

The hero is one who is transformed as the story progresses - the Customer is the hero going through a transformation. In the ad you need a hero, a goal, an obstacle, a mentor (the company) and a moral. The customer should know or have a feeling of empowerment. Therefore, encountering your company or product should add and build value to their experience, rather than dictating what they should do. You can get customers to react with a call to action such as "Sign up for a webinar" or "Take the next step". Marketing therefore effectively helps customers to become the hero of their lives by calling them to action.

STORYBOARDING

The storyboard and the empathy map help to further highlight the consumer's problem and the journey he/she must take to resolve it. Therefore, Journey mapping is also a form of story boarding. As a result, you'll build the customer's story by using the information you have gleaned from researching the target market. You can start with the end and move back to the beginning - lots of movies follow this model. Storyboards are used as a communication tool or springboard to flesh out the full story.

**An example of the storyboard
for Deber Collection of Yum**

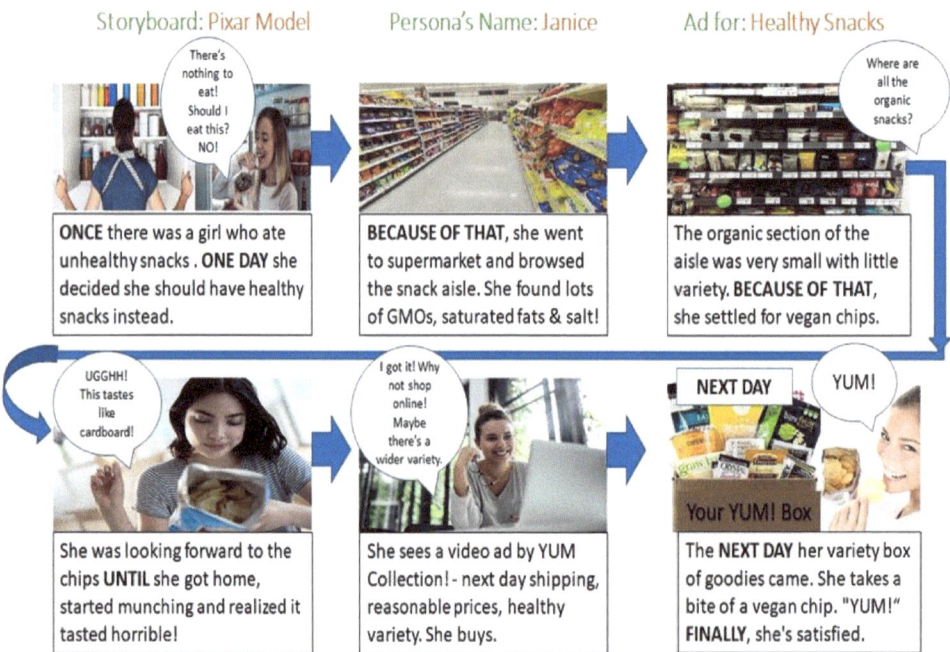

Exercise

1. Gather the information from the empathy map for this exercise.
2. Start with a template – whether you'll use the Pixar Model or the Hero's Journey Model.
3. Your story can end with a Call to action – so decide if you want your consumer to BUY NOW, SIGN UP for more information, or MAKE AN APPOINTMENT, depending on the model.
4. Keep your storyboard to 6 Frames and add content to each frame – like a graphic novel or a comic book. Decide on your story.

Tools & Resources

1. Marker and whiteboard.
2. Pen and paper.
3. Storyboards are the skeletons of your story, and they are simple, not complex. They are later developed in an app or platform for presentation. For example, you can use platform UX Storyboards for storytelling - UX (user experience).
4. To create the story, you can use Getty Images (gettyimages.com), or your own illustrations with the conversation bubble as used in graphic novels and comics.

CHAPTER 6
CUSTOMER ENGAGEMENT – THE ART OF STORYTELLING

Since marketing is the introduction of your product or service to your intended target audience, the two main important components in this mix are what you have to offer (product/service), and to whom you are offering it to (target customer). While the 4Ps of marketing (product, place, promotion, and price) are key to a good marketing mix, they would not exist without having a product or service and a target market to sell it to. Therefore, this makes the product or service and its target market the two most critical elements that can determine the success of a business.

Companies like Amazon, Google and Microsoft fully understand the significance of these elements and how they play a fundamental role in business strategy, growth, and profitability. They understand that meeting customers' needs and providing the right service or product to do so, is paramount to having the competitive edge and relevance while satisfying the consumer. It is within this combination that marketing becomes essential and effective, as the brand is aligned to the market's needs to build a strong, sustainable brand and enjoy long-term success in the marketplace.

Having the right market fit allows companies to market their brand to a more receptive audience. This leads to a deeper understanding of how to communicate to the target market. Marketing has no hard-and-fast rules. Therefore, by having the right combination of product and consumers, companies must continually adapt and refine their offerings to keep customers satisfied, and this also means adapting its communication to gain customer loyalty and repeat business.

However, for companies to successfully achieve this, they must develop the art of storytelling. In the last chapter we highlighted the foundations of storytelling – applying specific techniques (The Pixar Model and The Hero's Journey Model). In this chapter, we will look at customer engagement. Using storytelling prompts formulated by ChatGPT for various industries and on various selling platforms, business owners can ask questions to expand their brand's market share and explore ideas to generate customer engagement and retention more effectively.

Exercise
1. For this exercise, industries we chose for ChatGPT prompts are fashion and digital products on Etsy selling platform. However, you should use these prompts according to your product, selling platform, and customers, and design your own customer engagement outline and brand expansion profile.
2. Remember, the emotional connection with your customer is very important.
3. **See Chapter 10 to learn how to utilize ChatGPT.**

Tools & Resources
Prompts (ideas and questions) using ChatGPT: chat.openai.com

HOW TO KEEP YOUR CUSTOMERS ENGAGED WITH STORYTELLING TECHNIQUES USING AI

+

100 CHATGPT STORYTELLING PROMPT IDEAS!

Brand Storytelling is the art of humanizing your brand. This is done to connect with customers on a deeper level, and to share the brand's passion and dedication behind its product or service.

It's about creating a story or a narrative that customers relate to. Included in this narrative are the values, mission and aspirations of the brand that resonate with the values, mission, and aspirations of the target market. The brand will forge profound connections with consumers, consequently cultivating consumer loyalty.

STORYTELLING IDEAS FOR BLOGGING

Here are 10 Storytelling ChatGPT Blogging idea prompts for a DIGITAL PRODUCT COMPANY to engage its audience on ETSY.

1. Origins of Creativity: "Share the story of the very first digital product you created for Etsy. What inspired it, and how did it feel to launch it into the digital marketplace?"

2. Behind the Design: "Take us behind the scenes of your creative process. How do you come up with unique digital product ideas, and what's your favorite part of the design journey?"

3. Customer Tales: "Highlight a memorable customer story. How did your digital product make a difference in their life or project? We'd love to hear their experience!"

4. Seasonal Inspiration: "How do seasons and holidays inspire your digital product designs? Share a seasonal story that influenced one of your best-selling items."

5. Milestone Moments: "Celebrate a significant milestone in your Etsy journey. Whether it's your 100th sale or a special collaboration, tell us the story behind it."

6. Meet the Maker: "Introduce yourself! Share your personal journey, your passions outside of digital products, and how they influence your creations."

7. From Sketch to Sale: "Pick one of your digital products and walk us through its evolution, from the initial idea or sketch to the final listing on Etsy."

8. Behind the Shop Name: "What's the story behind your Etsy shop's name? Does it have a special meaning or connection to your products?"

9. Creative Challenges: "Every artist faces creative challenges. Share a story about a tough creative problem you encountered and how you overcame it."

10. Future Dreams: "Paint a picture of your future Etsy shop. What exciting new digital products or goals do you have in mind for your customers?"

NARRATIVE STRUCTURE

The typical brand storytelling idea often follows a narrative structure, like a storybook, with a protagonist (the brand or its customers), a conflict or challenge, and a resolution. Companies often use this structure in TV and video ads. Customers find this structure relatable, but not all brand storytelling follows this structure. This kind of structure also has a character, a moral, and of course a Call to Action at the end.

When writing your brand's Blog or Social Media posts, you can opt to tell a bit of story about your brand, by using the structure highlighted here, and the prompt ideas on the previous page to begin.

Imagine you're a digital product company. In your storyline, you can choose to appeal to the professional teacher or woman (the protagonist) who needs download printables or online forms and charts (the resolution) to assist her with her daily tasks (the challenge). Your company offers the solution.

THE STORY STRUCTURE - GET CUSTOMERS TO SHARE

Listed below are 10 Storytelling Structure ChatGPT prompts for a DIGITAL COMPANY to actively engage its customers.

These storytelling prompts can be used to invite customers to tell their story about the brand, thereby actively engaging your community.

1. User Spotlight: "Tell us your story! Share how our digital product has made a positive impact on your life or business. We'd love to feature your success story."
2. Behind-the-Scenes: "Take a virtual tour of our digital company! Meet our team, see our workspace, and learn about the creative process behind our products."
3. Product Evolution: "Explore the journey of one of our digital products. How has it evolved over time, and what inspired its development? Share its story with our customers."
4. Customer Challenges: "We all face digital challenges. Share a personal or professional obstacle you've encountered and how our product helped you overcome it."
5. Innovation Story: "Get an exclusive look into our latest innovation. What inspired its creation, and how will it revolutionize the digital landscape? Be among the first to hear the story behind it."
6. Community Impact: "Our digital community is a force for good. Share how our products have been used to benefit your community or support a cause close to your heart."
7. Digital Trends: "Explore the latest digital trends with us. How are emerging technologies shaping our digital world, and what role do our products play in these trends?"
8. Customer Collaborations: "Let's co-create! Share your ideas for improving our digital products. Your input matters, and we want to hear your innovative suggestions."
9. Digital Transformation: "Experience a digital transformation journey. Follow a customer's path from initial challenges to successful implementation of our products."
10. Digital Discovery: "Discover the hidden gems in our digital product portfolio. Dive into the stories behind lesser-known products and their unique features."

EMOTIONAL CONNECTION

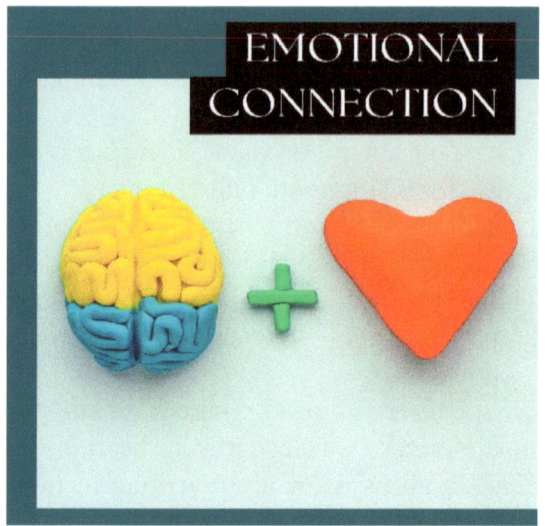

Storytelling evokes a variety of emotions, ranging from joy, sadness, inspiration, empathy and even nostalgia. It allows the brand to connect on a deeper level as the consumer relates via emotion, and as a result, the brand becomes reliable and trustworthy in the eyes of its consumers. Imagine a fashion brand wanting to connect with its followers and appeal to a more environmentally conscious audience with its new 100% cotton products. The brand would highlight and discuss topics such as the importance of sustainable fashion and eco-friendly clothing in its blog and social media posts. It may also choose to inform the audience about its reduced carbon footprint and its positive impact on the environment to emotionally connect with its new target market.

CONNECTING EMOTIONALLY VIA SOCIAL MEDIAL DISCUSSIONS

Listed below are 10 storytelling prompts for a FASHION BRAND to evoke an emotional connection with its audience:

1. Fashion Journey: "Share a personal fashion journey with us. Describe a memorable outfit or accessory that made you feel confident and empowered. What's the story behind it?"
2. Transformation Tale: "Fashion has the power to transform. Tell us about a significant moment in your life where the right outfit made all the difference. How did it impact your emotions and confidence?"
3. Iconic Style Moments: "Reflect on iconic fashion moments in history. Which style icons or fashion eras have influenced your personal style and emotional connection to fashion?"
4. Fashion and Memories: "Our clothes often hold memories. Share a cherished memory associated with a particular fashion piece or accessory. What emotions does it bring back?"
5. Sustainability Story: "Discuss the emotional importance of sustainable fashion. How does choosing eco-friendly clothing make you feel, and what impact do you believe it has on the world?"
6. Fashion as Self-Expression: "Fashion is a form of self-expression. Describe how your style choices reflect your personality and values. How does fashion empower you to be yourself?"
7. Fashion Icons: "Highlight a fashion icon who inspires you. What is it about their style or attitude that resonates with you emotionally?"
8. Fashion and Confidence: "Explore the link between fashion and confidence. Share a story of how wearing a particular outfit boosted your self-confidence and influenced your day."
9. Fashion for Special Occasions: "Recall a special occasion where choosing the perfect outfit was emotionally significant. How did your outfit enhance the event's experience?"
10. Fashion Resolutions: "As we step into a new season or year, what fashion resolutions or style goals do you have? How do you envision these changes impacting your emotional well-being?"

How can your
brand extend
beyond your
product, logo,
website, etc.?

Consider reaching
your brand across
many networks
and global fronts.

Next, learn how to
extend your brand
to far-reaching
audiences.

BRANDING THAT EXTENDS BEYOND.

Customizing the ChatGPT prompts for brand extension to suit your brand's unique identity and goals is the key to successfully expand your fashion brand into several markets. Growing a fashion brand online requires a strategic combination of digital marketing, a strong online presence, engaging with your target audience and possibly new markets, while keeping up with consumer trends and preferences. Brand extension includes the following:

- Online Presence. Customer engagement.
- Brand Expansion.
- Marketing Strategies.
- E-commerce and Sales.
- Fashion Trends and Innovation.

Listed are the ChatGPT prompts for each segment to facilitate growth and expansion for your fashion brand.

ONLINE PRESENCE

How can you use ChatGPT to improve your online presence? What questions should you ask to get the most relatable answers? Listed below are the Top 10 Online Presence ChatGPT prompts to facilitate a fashion brand expansion:

1. "How can I ensure that my fashion products align with my brand. What social media platforms are most effective for promoting a fashion brand?"
2. "How can I optimize my website for search engines (SEO) to increase online visibility?"
3. "Provide tips on creating engaging content for my fashion brand's blog."
4. "What are effective strategies for growing my brand's email subscriber list?"
5. "Suggest ways to leverage influencer marketing to promote my fashion brand."
6. "How can I use social media advertising to reach a larger audience?"
7. "What should be my approach to online customer reviews and testimonials?"
8. "Share ideas for hosting virtual fashion events to showcase my products."
9. "How can I use email marketing to nurture customer relationships and drive sales?"
10. "What are the benefits of using user-generated content in my online branding efforts?"

CUSTOMER ENGAGEMENT

How can you use ChatGPT to help in improving customer engagement and retention? Listed below are the Top 10 Customer Engagement ChatGPT prompts:

1. "What are effective strategies for engaging with customers on social media?"
2. "Suggest ways to create an online fashion community around my brand."
3. "How can I use storytelling to connect with my audience and build brand loyalty?"
4. "Provide ideas for running social media contests or giveaways to engage customers."
5. "What should be my approach to handling customer inquiries and feedback?"
6. "Share tips for building trust and credibility with online customers."

7. "How can I use customer-generated content to showcase real experiences with my brand?"
8. "What strategies can I implement to encourage user reviews and testimonials?"
9. "Help me brainstorm customer retention strategies for my fashion brand."
10. "How can I gather and use customer data to improve my brand's online presence?"

BRAND EXPANSION

How can you use ChatGPT to help in the expansion of your brand? Listed below are the Top 10 Brand Expansion ChatGPT prompts for fashion branding:

1. "Suggest strategies for expanding my fashion brand into international markets."
2. "What are the benefits of collaborating with other fashion brands or designers?"
3. "Provide ideas for launching a new product line that complements my existing offerings."
4. "How can I explore the potential of brick-and-mortar retail or pop-up shops?"
5. "What should be my approach to wholesale partnerships and distribution?"
6. "Help me understand the role of affiliate marketing in expanding my brand."
7. "Share tips for utilizing email campaigns to announce brand expansion initiatives."
8. "What are effective strategies for entering the luxury fashion market?"
9. "How can I create buzz and anticipation around upcoming brand developments?"
10. "Suggest ways to leverage strategic alliances or sponsorships for brand growth."

BRAND REPUTATION MANAGEMENT

Questions to ask ChatGPT about improving brand management. Listed below are the Top 10 ChatGPT prompts that will help you with Brand Management:

1. "What steps can I take to protect my fashion brand's intellectual property and trademarks?"
2. "How should I handle negative press or online criticism related to my brand?"
3. "Provide advice on crisis management and communication in the fashion industry."
4. "What strategies can I use to maintain a positive online reputation for my brand?"
5. "Help me understand the importance of social responsibility and brand ethics."
6. "Share tips for addressing product recalls or quality issues transparently."
7. "How can I effectively address customer concerns and complaints to protect my brand?"
8. "Suggest ways to showcase my brand's commitment to sustainability and environmental responsibility."
9. "What should be my approach to brand transparency and disclosure of practices?"
10. "Provide ideas for leveraging positive customer stories and brand successes."

MARKETING STRATEGIES

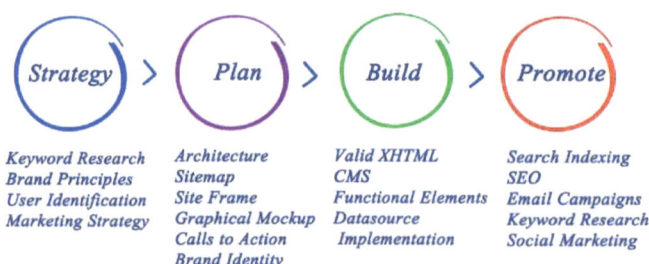

Get some new ideas about marketing your product or service. Listed below are the Top 10 ChatGPT Marketing Strategy prompts for fashion businesses.

1. "What are effective strategies for launching a fashion brand on social media from scratch?"
2. "How can I use Instagram to showcase my fashion brand's lifestyle and values?"

3. "Suggest creative ideas for using video marketing to promote my brand."
4. "Share tips on creating compelling product videos for online marketing."
5. "What should be my approach to using Instagram Stories and Reels for brand promotion?"
6. "Provide insights on the role of Pinterest in driving traffic and sales for fashion brands."
7. "How can I leverage TikTok to engage with a younger audience for my brand?"
8. "Suggest email marketing campaigns to build anticipation for product launches."
9. "What are effective strategies for using influencer collaborations in fashion marketing?"
10. "Help me understand the potential of content marketing and blogging for my brand."

ECOMMERCE & SALES

e-Commerce is a very powerful tool that can quickly expand your brand to several markets worldwide.

Use ChatGPT to provide ideas to effectively scale your ecommerce business. Listed below are the Top 10 ChatGPT E-Commerce & Sales prompts for fashion brands:

1. "What e-commerce platforms are best suited for selling fashion products online?"
2. "How can I optimize my product listings on e-commerce platforms for better sales?"
3. Suggest strategies for using limited time offers and flash sales to boost revenue."
4. "Share tips for creating a seamless and user-friendly online shopping experience."
5. "What should be my approach to upselling and cross-selling fashion products?"
6. "Provide ideas for using online advertising to drive traffic and sales."
7. "How can I implement an effective abandoned cart recovery strategy?"
8. "Suggest strategies for managing inventory and handling product availability."
9. "What are effective tactics for offering excellent customer service in e-commerce?"
10. "Help me understand the role of data analytics in optimizing my online sales."

FASHION TRENDS & INNOVATION

How about following the latest trends in your industry? Use ChatGPT to determine how you can keep ahead. Listed below are the Top 10 Fashion Trends & Innovation ChatGPT prompts for fashion brand expansion.

1. "How can I stay updated on the latest fashion trends and industry developments?"
2. "Suggest ways to incorporate sustainable and eco-friendly practices into my brand."
3. "What role does technology play in the future of fashion, and how can I adapt?"
4. "Provide insights on the impact of AI and data analytics in fashion branding."
5. "How can I use 3D printing or virtual fashion experiences to differentiate my brand?"
6. "Share ideas for collaborating with emerging fashion designers or artists."
7. "What are the potential benefits of creating a limited-edition fashion collection?"
8. "Help me understand the importance of size inclusivity and diversity in fashion."
9. "Suggest strategies for aligning my brand with current cultural or societal movements."
10. "How can I foster innovation and creativity within my fashion brand for long-term growth?"

Disclaimer: Please note that some information provided by ChatGPT may not be accurate as the data is being pulled from different sources on the Internet. Please make sure to Fact-Check information before using it, as well as rewrite or rephrase information that will be used in blogs, newsletters, etc., to avoid plagiarism.

Imagine the kinds of questions you can ask or the types of prompts you can generate to cultivate success online, to improve your brand's reputation, and to keep customers engaged.

Don't forget the more you customize your ChatGPT prompts, the more tailored the responses will be.

_____

_____

_____

_____

_____

_____

_____

_____

_____

_____

_____

_____

_____

_____

_____

_____

_____

_____

CHAPTER 7
KEY COMPONENTS FOR MARKETING YOUR BRAND ONLINE

There are several key components to building a brand that is marketable online. These factors work well together, and they facilitate tremendous success in this digital age.

These are core values (some of which we have already covered) that every business (not just those online) should have at its foundation.

1. Identify your SKEPT (Skill, Knowledge, Experience, Passion and Talent). That is, how can you or your company meet the need of others by utilizing what you know? *(Tjibaria, FLC, 2020)*.
2. Create a relatable logo and tagline. This should embody your brand's mission.
3. Create your Brand's DNA, key qualities and benefits your brand offers; state your Brand Position Statement; decide on your Target Market; determine your brand's Market Landscape and Advantage by creating a SWOT Analysis; and provide your customers with a Reason to Believe in your brand.
4. Automate your product or service using digital platforms, which enables your customers to have easy access to your offer.
5. Digital Marketing. Be visible and passionate about your purpose. Being visible both online and offline helps others to know about you, and being passionate about your brand adds value to your message.

This may sound like a lot of steps, and you may feel overwhelmed at first, but once you begin, you'll realize that the journey is an exciting one. Remember to have fun while doing this! It's also an eye–opening process – you may learn a thing or two about yourself or your company's mission!

Meet Your Customer's Needs by Utilizing What You Know

Tjibaria, FLC, 2020.

Q. How can your brand's mission statement be brought to life with SKEPT?

A. Each of us are driven by our skills, knowledge, experience, passion and talent. Imagine how you can employ these traits into your brand!

Skill

Humans tend to employ the skills they possess in everything they do. It's only natural we want to showcase our skills also in our businesses. Branding is no exception to this rule. Showcasing your skills and creativity in your business can help you stand out in your industry. Here are some ways design can help you showcase your skills:

- Strengthen your brand identity with a unique logo, color scheme, and even the typography (fonts) you use.
- Be creative in the graphics and visuals you use in your marketing materials to build customer awareness and attention.
- The same goes for your social media posts to promote your business and engage with your customers.
- Most businesses forget about product packaging, but this is another way to reflect the brand and stand apart from your competitors.

Knowledge

What you know is important. Knowledge about your product, service and industry is vital to the success of your business. Having a deeper understanding can help you make informed decisions, anticipate market trends, and stay ahead of the competition. It can also help you identify new opportunities for growth and innovation. A strong knowledge base can increase your credibility – your customers will see you are an expertise in your field, and this builds trust, leading to increased loyalty and repeat business (customer retention).

So, keep learning and staying up to date with the latest developments in your field to maintain a competitive edge and achieve long-term success.

Experience

Nothing like utilizing your prior work experience in your business. Drawing from your past work experience can be an asset. Here are some ways that your prior work experience can be utilized:

- Apply skills and knowledge gained from previous jobs to your business, such as project management, problem-solving, and communication skills.
- Such skills can help you in your communication to customers, identify potential clients and target markets.
- Leverage your network (who you know) from previous jobs to build relationships, promote your brand and generate leads for your business.
- Having experience in your area of business can be an advantage in your industry, especially if you have specialized knowledge or expertise.
- Prior work experience can be used to create case studies or testimonials to showcase your skills, capabilities, and expertise to potential clients.

Passion

It's said that what we love is what we do best. Bringing your passion for your work helps to make a successful business. It drives innovation and creativity, leading to new ideas and solutions, and it's because you're doing what you love. Imagine the motivation and commitment you can bring to your business when passion is employed. It will help you to stay focused about your brand's vision.

Also, your passion transcends your team, inspiring and energizing them, and creating a productive work environment.

Customers can feel the passion of your brand too through a strong brand identity. When customers resonate with your brand, it leads to customer loyalty and trust, as they see your genuine commitment to the value you place in your product or service.

Passion helps to drive your business to success.

Talent

Talent, like knowledge, is a key component in showcasing your brand to the target market.

Customers appreciate well-made products and innovative services that meet their needs and desires.

The ability to create helps to communicate your brand's message and ensures your brand is represented in the best possible way in which customers will appreciate your unique offer.

As we have now cleared #s 1-3 off our list (see page 36), let's delve more into the core values of marketing (#s 4&5).

CHAPTER 8
SOCIAL MEDIA PLATFORMS

I mentioned before, your brand image should be consistent for an effective marketing strategy. This includes being consistent across all social media platforms.

Naturally then, the logo and the tagline will be the same on Facebook, Instagram, Twitter, LinkedIn and wherever else you want to place your brand. Therefore, the social media profile will have the same information; whether it's for personal or business branding.

BUILDING AN AUDIENCE FROM SCRATCH

*Neil Patel (Online Marketer) believes that you can build an audience and grow your business by engaging one-on-one with readers on your blog, YouTube, etc. Also, you should find out what they have read, and guest post on these sites; plus ask members in your community to share, use links of leaders or mention their data in your blog post and ask them to share your blog with their followers. Building an audience from scratch takes consistency and dedication:

1. Decide to be a leader on a new medium or an existing social network.
2. Diversify into other markets and social media, consider other platforms.
3. Another way to build is through incentives, reward programs - a loyalty program.
4. Provide exclusive and consistent content – being present online frequently builds awareness. This is known as Organic Marketing. Use Constant-Content.com for customized or ready-made SEO-friendly blog posts, videos, white papers, etc. Good content makes organic marketing very effective as it encourages viewer engagement.
5. PR and guerrilla marketing (creating a marketing campaign to build awareness, and flash mobs helps marketers to piggyback off the buzz of an existing campaign). Guerrilla marketing is edgy and can break some rules and so therefore it could be risky. It's also known as ambush marketing and should be weighed heavily because it's all about making fun of the competition or piggybacking off the competitor's ads in order to garner the same kind of market attention.
6. Direct marketing or email marketing is very effective as the consumer is required to provide his/her email information in exchange for filling out a survey sampling or to ascertain a discount offer. Online marketing tools such as Mailchimp provide all-in-one business and marketing from websites, design tools and templates, to reward tools and automated email marketing campaigns.
7. Experiential marketing refers to giving customers a memorable buying experience. Free trials, samples and testing are examples of experiential marketing. Being consistent on social media also helps in this kind of marketing strategy, as you make yourself available to answer questions and queries and talk freely about your goods and/or services.

All of this entails building an audience from scratch (organic marketing). While it takes time, it is very effective. This is where companies get to know their target audience and keep their consumers engaged.

Tools & Resources

*Neil Patel (Online Marketer & YouTuber): neilpatel.com

Email Marketing: Mailchimp.com

Online Content: Constant-content.com

CHAPTER 9
YOUR DIGITAL MARKETING SHOULD STRENGTHEN YOUR BRAND

There are many ways to grow and strengthen your brand. However, your strategies and techniques should be planned and timed strategically.

THE MARKETING PLAN - usually considers the company's goals and highlights the objectives of the marketing team to accomplish these goals.

Creating a Digital Marketing Plan:

1. Begin with objectives & goals. These should be SMART; that is, you should identify and discover components of the digital marketing plan, explore roles in digital marketing and do your research. SMART goals are as follows: **S** - Specific - what, why, who, where - your objective should not be vague (like I want to produce good quality products) - a more specific objective is focusing on a specific product for a targeted region. **M** - Measurable - metrics, milestones, results, budget, completed task or accomplished objective - what are the current key performances? **A** - Achievable - skill, resources, tools, time - do I have these resources to accomplish these constraints; is it realistic? **R** - Relevant - need, objectives, values, goals - what you're trying to achieve, is it relevant to your company's need, objectives, and goals, and does it bring relevant value to the consumer? Are your objectives applicable? **T** - Time-bound - an objective that can be achieved within a set timeframe. Create focused milestones and deadlines for your objectives. **You should really take the time to answer these questions to determine how, when, where and who to market to.**
2. Conduct a SWOT Analysis. A SWOT Analysis is important as it allows the company to determine its inner strengths and weaknesses and the external opportunities and threats that may affect the brand.

SWOT Analysis for Deber Collection of Yum

Strengths:

- Provides healthier snacking options for customers.
- Authenticity and reliability in the company's product sourcing.
- Online retailing and accessible care packages that can be delivered world-wide.

Weaknesses:

- The company needs a more solid marketing strategy.
- More effective execution of marketing plans.

Opportunities:

- Future opportunity to offer monthly subscription boxes of a variety of snacks, teas and brews. This niche is under-represented.
- Covid-19 provides an opportunity to build customer awareness and expand market share.
- Possible future sourcing of foreign snack imports into the US market.

Threats:

- Although not necessarily providing healthy snacks, there are other online retailers who offer subscription boxes with a significant market share in this niche. Major online subscription retailers are KIND Snacks, SnackSack, My Keto Snack Box and Mexicrate.

3. Choose digital marketing tactics – This could be focused on awareness if the company is new; or on expanding target market, and marketing channels, if the company is in its growth stage.
4. A marketing budget must be set, and results must be measured (set KPI for sales, awareness increase, survey responses, social media follow base, customer feedback on experience, customer retention). You can also do a competitive Analysis (measure what your competitors' marketing plan against your own) after a marketing plan has been instituted.
5. Pilot testing/Concept Testing – This is running a campaign to a smaller group and if it's successful and conversion rate of sampling is good, the campaign can be done on a grander scale.

Remember, the digital marketing strategy should be a 360-degree strategy.

BUILDING ORGANIC TRAFFIC

1. Improve organic traffic by improving SEO, posting on social media, blogging and by using hashtags. Hashtags help you to see what other people are posting about and also help to bring awareness to your post.
2. Organic traffic builds awareness by creating engagement; thereby, lowering the website's bounce rate. Customers visiting other pages on the website show interest.
3. Encourage others to hashtag your brand name to build awareness. One way to measure reach is looking at the number of impressions and the number of followers and email opt-ins or the percentage of RoI – return on investment. This information is available on the back end of either your website or landing page.
4. Discount codes are also a great way to measure conversion and efficacy, and they can be used offline.
5. Create video content to drive organic traffic. Use action words, keep it simple and to the point. Keep in mind most marketing videos are 5 seconds to 1 minute. Interactive videos that get the customer to engage in a task, such as those used on Vimeo, are fresh and new.

Finally, create a basic tool that people can use – this is a great way to drive traffic to your site. For example, Deber Collection of Yum would add an Ad plug-in to its website, such as a quiz about healthy snacks. This quiz would be uploaded to social media to drive people back to the brand's website – any data collected can later become blog content or topic for discussion on social media posts., thereby generating more customer awareness and engagement – this is a 360-degree strategy.

Tools & Resources
SMART Goals Framework: Hubspot.com
SWOT Analysis Template: Creately.com
Vimeo Videomaking: Vimeo.com

List your SMART goals. They should align with the mission and vision of your brand.

_____

_____

_____

_____

_____

_____

_____

_____

_____

_____

_____

_____

_____

_____

_____

_____

_____

_____

_____

CHAPTER 10
INTERNET HACKS (FUNNELS & AI)

Funnels

The product's website is not the only way to arrest the customer's attention. Creating a landing page for a funnel is an ingenious way for more content-focused and targeted marketing.

Of course, for online businesses, meeting the audience where they are located (online) is paramount. This is why funnels are important. They pull the customer into a landing page and channel them through a streamlined process toward your desired objective. The desired goal may be website or product awareness, prelaunch, or sign-up process for leads or sales. Therefore, there are different kinds of funnels which allow marketers to achieve different objectives:

> ➤ The Opt-in Funnel – This allows customers to opt-in to an offer. The funnel collects important information such as the customer's name and email address; thereby resulting in leads for the marketer. The Opt-in Funnel allows marketers to create brand awareness and build customer loyalty.
> ➤ Purchase Funnel – In this funnel, the company provides content-focused information about the product they wish customers to purchase. The funnel's pop up captures the customer's information, leading them to the sales page. If the product is placed and abandoned in the shopping cart, then a reminder email and a discount or price drop is sent to the customer.
> ➤ Cross Sell Funnel – Marketers can sell more than one product by stating "Customers who bought this also bought this". This is done by moving the customer through the funnel from one page to the next.
> ➤ Up Sell Funnel – Here is an opportunity to buy more, or a pack, or to get a discount if customers subscribe, opt-in for an automatic annual renewal, etc. Up sell funnels are used to increase sale opportunities.

NOTE: companies use funnels to sell their main product (their big-ticket item) by enticing consumers with similar items with less cost (small-ticket items) or with free giveaways (opt-in products).

The greatest thing about funnels is that they provide accurate analytics and insight into conversion rates. The top of the funnel, being wider, indicates the place where all customers meet to visit the website, and as they move from the landing page to the opt-in, up sell or cross sell pages, the funnel gets narrower as only the customers who are more interested in what you have to offer move further through down into the rabbit hole (through your funnel pages and onto the other side of buy cart). Very cool digital innovation, as it provides a clearer picture of customers who are serious about your product or service, and the ones who are just browsing.

NOTE: Don't rule out the customers who are browsing. They are considered as leads; that is, possible future prospects/customers. Through your upsell, opt-in or cross-sell pages, one day their browsing may become conversion. The benefit of funnels is that the marketer can track every detail of his/her marketing efforts, from leads to conversions.

AI (Artificial Intelligence) Including ChatGPT

There are several kinds of artificial intelligence available on the internet. Many can be used for branding and marketing purposes. This means that businesses can utilize these advanced technologies to improve how they present their products or services to the public. These AI tools have a wide range of capabilities. They can analyze people's feelings about a product, predict future market trends, suggest personalized choices, and even create web pages and social media content automatically. By employing these AI solutions, companies can increase their brand's visibility, fine-tune their marketing tactics, and establish stronger connections with their intended target market. As a result, these technologies are reshaping the way modern advertising and promotions are approached. Imagine using artificial intelligence (AI) for your branding and marketing needs – this takes the guess work out of who to target to, what product is trending, price-point entry for your intended market, and provides more accurate data for analytics.

Here are some examples of how to employ AI for your branding and marketing solutions:

1. **Chatbots and Virtual Assistants**: These AI-driven tools can provide real-time customer support, answer queries, and guide users through the buying process. They enhance user experience and engagement, creating a positive brand impression. Chatbots can be used to interact with customers on your website (front end), while Virtual Assistants can be installed in the admin panel (back end) of your website to help you with automatic marketing campaigns, creating web content and providing analytics. One good AI to use is MailChimp, which is a Virtual Assistant that can fulfill these needs. MailChimp is great for email marketing to specific target markets at a time, as well as providing accurate and detailed data analytics. You can also include *Siri, Cortana, Alexa and Google Assistant.*

2. **Personalization Engines**: AI algorithms, like those used in the back end of Netflix' and Amazon's websites, analyze user data to deliver tailored recommendations and content to customers. These algorithms help to provide a more personalized user experience, thereby building strong customer relationships and increasing conversions. Personalization engines are usually built into the templates of ready-made e-Commerce websites such as *Shopify, Wix, and SquareSpace.*

3. **Analysis & Analytics**: AI can analyze the public by gauging the sentiment of social media and online content for your brand or product. AI can predict consumer behavior based on historical data gathered from your website (data analytics). This helps marketers make informed decisions on product launches, pricing, and promotional activities. Both are usually built-ins or add-on plugins on most e-Commerce websites.

4. **Content Generation:** AI-powered tools can generate written content, such as blog posts, social media updates, and product descriptions, saving time and resources while maintaining a consistent brand voice. ChatGPT is ideal for providing prompts, suggestions, and written content.

5. **Image and Video Recognition:** AI can identify brand logos, products, or even specific scenes in images and videos. According to Sprout Social (Repustate, 2021) and Conner (2019), companies do this to monitor their brand and content, and to analyze how they are being used and perceived by customers. You can use the free **Google Image Recognition**

service by simply asking Google about the company's logo, then click on "Images" or "Videos" below the Google Search Box.

6. **Social Media Management**: AI tools can schedule social media posts, analyze engagement metrics, and even respond to user comments, streamlining social media marketing efforts. Here's a current and detailed list of AI software recommended by Rebelo (2023) at Zapier Inc. You can view list here (or see Reference page for full link address). This also includes automated digital advertising campaigns and suggestive ad creatives based on real-time performance data.

7. **Automation**: Most companies use Zapier as their automated tool that connects the different apps they use in one space, such as Facebook, Instagram and Mailchimp. It connects two or more apps to trigger actions based on specific events happening on your company's website such as a purchase. It then creates an automation process such as a social media mention on Instagram or an email marketing campaign on MailChimp. Zapier employs repetitive tasks and processes that involve multiple apps.

ChatGPT for Branding and Digital Marketing

"ChatGPT for Marketing" is designed to assist with various digital marketing tasks, including content generation, social media management, email drafting, and more. It leverages natural language processing to understand user inputs and provide relevant and detailed and summarized responses, depending on your needs. It is an asset for digital marketers looking to streamline their workflows and enhance their content both on- and offline.

NOTE: *Please keep in mind, to date (at the writing of this book in 2023), ChatGPT's data has only been updated to September 2021. Therefore, current or real-time data will not be available or accessible in the ChatGPT app or website.*

You can utilize ChatGPT for the following marketing and branding solutions:

1. **Data Analysis and Insights:** ChatGPT can process large volumes of data to uncover your company's past trends, preferences, and customer behavior patterns, which can guide strategic marketing decisions. **NOTE:** This is ideal for companies which were formulated before September 2021 because the AI's data has only been updated to September 2021. However, if you needed information on your competitors and their past trends to help create your Brand Positioning and your Threats for your SWOT, this would be ideal.

2. **Influencer Suggestions:** ChatGPT can provide suggestions on the type of influencers you can use to promote your brand and for brand partnerships. For example, in your ChatGPT app, you can ask *"What type of influencers can I use to promote my sneaker brand?"* ChatGPT will immediately respond with several suggestions that are particularly selective for your brand.

3. **Language Translation for Various Global Markets:** The beauty of ChatGPT is it offers language translation that marketers can use to expand their reach and brand positioning.

4. **Brainstorm Ideas:** Use ChatGPT to brainstorm ideas on products and services you can provide either for a trending market or for a niche market. For example, ask for a list of ideas for your request, such as *"Give me 5 ideas for trending products to sell on eBay"*, or even step-by-step instructions such as *"Give me step-by-step instructions on how to list a product on eBay"*.

5. **Market Research:** Have ChatGPT analyze market trends, consumer sentiments, and competitor strategies through the use of comparative data analysis, to help determine your market entry (if you're just beginning) or refine your strategy in staying ahead in your industry.

6. **Content Creation:** ChatGPT shines in content creation, whether it's web content such as writing for blogs, newsletters, email marketing, and/or social media posts.

Tutorial - How to Use ChatGPT for Marketing

1. **Log in** at https://chat.openai.com

2. **Click Sign Up** and you can choose to do so via Google or you can manually type in your email address (which would require creating a password).

3. **Verify** your identity via entering the code sent to your phone number.

4. This will take you to ChatGPT's Dashboard.

5. You can start a new chat by clicking the + sign at the upper left corner of screen or by simply typing in the Search box at the bottom of the screen.

6. Keep in mind each New Chat is saved in the website or app's history.

7. **Train Your Bot.** By clicking the "thumbs-up" or "thumbs-down" icons and providing feedback, you are "training" your bot to give better answers. If something is incorrect, highlight and copy the incorrect sentence or paragraph, then click the thumbs down icon. It will ask for feedback. Paste the highlight in the box stating that the sentence or paragraph is incorrect. Maybe also include the correct answer.

8. **Summarized Research.** ChatGPT summarizes from various online sources to provide a creatively specific answer for your question or request. Ask anything:

what influencers can i use to promote my sneaker brand?

Selecting the right influencers to promote your sneaker brand depends on your target audience, brand identity, and marketing goals. Here are a few categories of influencers you might consider:

1. **Fashion and Lifestyle Influencers:** Collaborating with fashion and lifestyle influencers who have a strong following in the sneaker and streetwear niche can help you reach an audience that's already interested in your product category.
2. **Athletes and Sports Influencers:** If your sneaker brand focuses on performance or athletic footwear, partnering with athletes or sports influencers can lend credibility and appeal to individuals interested in fitness and sports.
3. **Sneaker Enthusiasts and Collectors:** Seek out influencers who are passionate about sneakers and have built a following around their sneaker collection and knowledge. Their authentic enthusiasm can resonate with fellow sneaker enthusiasts.

9. **Generate Several Responses.** Click "Regenerate Response" at the bottom of the screen to get more information. You can toggle back and forth between both answers by clicking the arrows of 2/2 (as seen below).

< 2/2

10. **Give a command.** This tells the bot what to do. For example, if you are creating a listing for your product online, ChatGPT can provide an expansion on your sentence or paragraph, after which you can adjust to suit your offer. Please note, to give a command, place a colon between the command and your description (as seen below). **Also, please remember to rewrite or rephrase generated prompts for creative writing or descriptions you will later use to avoid plagiarism.**

Expand this sentence for eBay listing: Free People H2O Crew Pullover, color Tiger Eye shade, size Large, long sleeve

Sure, here's an expanded sentence you can use for an eBay listing:

"Experience both comfort and style with the Free People H2O Crew Pullover in the captivating Tiger Eye shade. This pullover, crafted by Free People, renowned for their quality and unique designs, offers a blend of warmth and fashion. Sized as Large, this long-sleeved pullover ensures a relaxed fit that's perfect for layering or wearing on its own. The Tiger Eye color infuses a rich and earthy tone into your wardrobe, adding a touch of warmth to any outfit. Whether you're lounging at home or exploring the outdoors, this Free People H2O Crew Pullover combines a cozy feel with a trend-setting aesthetic."

Here's another example. Suppose you are selling scented candles, then your product appeals to young and older housewives and even single women. You give your ChatGPT bot the following command:

"Pretend you are a housewife. Create an outline for various blog ideas that are fun and casual for candles written in the voice of a housewife.". Notice we are trying to appeal to the demographic to which we are marketing. To get a good result, tell ChatGPT to "Pretend" who it should be. Here, we are asking for blog ideas for a specific niche, and ChatGPT provided the topics as well as several subtopics that would appeal to the intended target market. From these subtopics you can create several different blog posts which would keep your audience engaged.

Remember your commands should be very specific and to the point, and in the tone you want (such as energetic, business-like, casual, etc.).

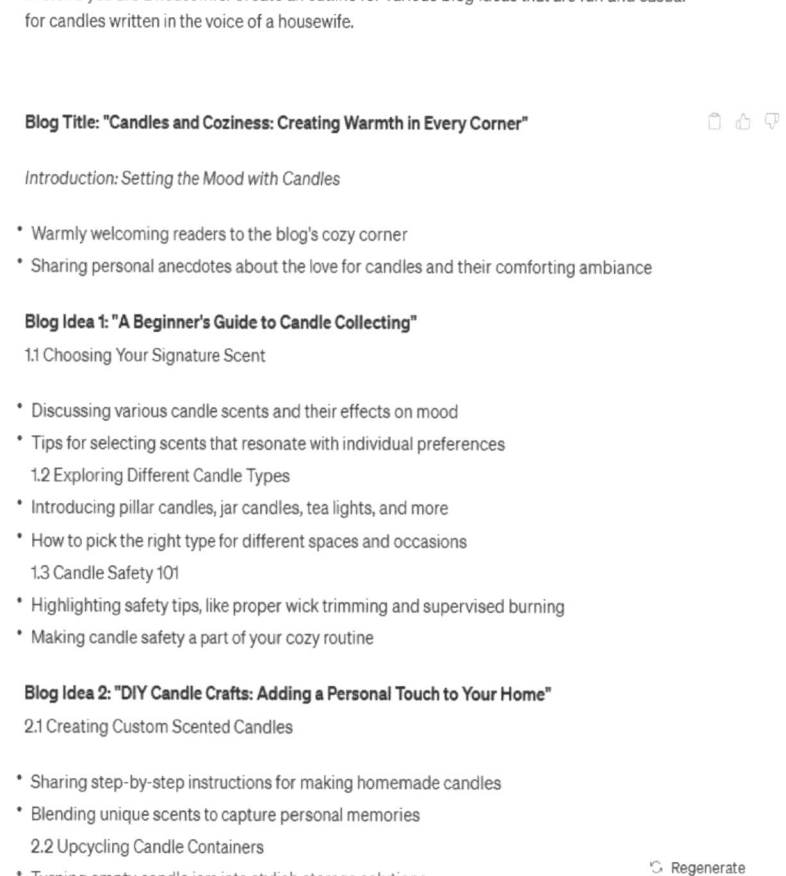

Keep in mind too that you can brainstorm for video ideas for short videos to promote your brand on Instagram, Facebook Reels, and YouTube Shorts, as well as scripts for email marketing and eye-catching email subject headings!

11. **Translate.** To reach global markets, you can use ChatGPT's language translation. For example, if we wanted the below eBay listing to expand to the Korean market on eBay, we would command our bot to convert the listing into Korean. This can also be done for social media, blogs, etc.

> Translate this into Korean: "Experience both comfort and style with the Free People H2O Crew Pullover in the captivating Tiger Eye shade. This pullover, crafted by Free People, renowned for their quality and unique designs, offers a blend of warmth and fashion. Sized as Large, this long-sleeved pullover ensures a relaxed fit that's perfect for layering or wearing on its own. The Tiger Eye color infuses a rich and earthy tone into your wardrobe, adding a touch of warmth to any outfit. Whether you're lounging at home or exploring the outdoors, this Free People H2O Crew Pullover combines a cozy feel with a trend-setting aesthetic."

"편안함과 스타일을 모두 느껴보세요. 매혹적인 타이거 아이 컬러의 프리 피플 H2O 크루 풀오버와 함께 하세요. 이 풀오버는 프리 피플이 제작한 제품으로, 그들의 품질과 독특한 디자인으로 유명합니다. 따뜻함과 패션의 조화를 제공합니다. 사이즈는 **Large**로, 이 롱 슬리브 풀오버는 레이어링이나 단독 착용에 완벽한 여유로운 핏을 보장합니다. 타이거 아이 컬러는 풍부하고 토성 같은 톤을 옷장에 불어넣어 어떤 코디에도 따뜻함을 더합니다. 집에서 편안하게 놀거나 야외를 탐험하던 중이든, 이 프리 피플 H2O 크루 풀오버는 아늑함과 트렌드를 결합한 느낌을 전합니다."

12. **Compare.** When determining your Brand or Market Positioning, use ChatGPT to compare your competitors and markets. ChatGPT is a great feature to use for market trends, consumer behavior and market competition comparison. For example, see the comparison between Amazon's and eBay's 2019 Quarter 1 (January to March) overall performance, with command *"Compare Amazon 2019 Q1 performance with eBay 2019 Q1 performance"*.

Amazon 2019 Q1 Performance:

* **Revenue Growth:** In Q1 2019, Amazon reported strong revenue growth. The company's net sales increased compared to the same period in the previous year, driven by growth in its core e-commerce business, Amazon Web Services (AWS), and other segments.
* **Profitability:** Amazon reported a net income for the quarter, indicating profitability. However, Amazon often prioritizes growth over short-term profitability by reinvesting in various initiatives and expanding its services.
* **E-commerce Expansion:** Amazon continued to invest in its e-commerce operations, expanding its product offerings, improving delivery services, and enhancing the customer experience.
* **Amazon Web Services (AWS):** AWS, Amazon's cloud computing division, continued to be a major contributor to the company's overall revenue and profitability. AWS reported strong growth and maintained its position as a leader in the cloud services market.
* **International Operations:** Amazon's international operations faced challenges, including currency fluctuations and competition in certain markets.

eBay 2019 Q1 Performance:

* **Revenue:** eBay's revenue for Q1 2019 showed modest growth compared to the previous year. The company's marketplace platforms contributed the majority of its revenue.
* **Profitability:** eBay reported a net income for the quarter, indicating profitability. Like Amazon, eBay also focuses on enhancing its user experience and platform rather than solely on short-term profits.
* **Marketplace Focus:** eBay continued to refine its marketplace platform, including improvements to search functionality and user interfaces. The company also focused on attracting both buyers and sellers to its platform.
* **Payment Services:** In 2019, eBay was in the process of transitioning its payment processing away from PayPal to manage payments internally. This transition aimed to provide a seamless experience for users.

↻ Regenerate

13. **Brainstorm.** Use ChatGPT to brainstorm ideas on products and services you can provide either for a trending market or for a niche market by using commands such as *"Give me 5 ideas for trending products to sell on eBay"*, or to have more details, request step-by-step instructions such as *"Give me step-by-step instructions on how to list a product on eBay"*.

Give me step-by-step instructions on how to list a product on eBay

Sure, here's a step-by-step guide on how to list a product on eBay:

Step 1: Sign In or Create an Account
If you don't already have an eBay account, sign up for one. If you have an account, log in.

Step 2: Navigate to "Sell"
Click on the "Sell" option on the top navigation bar. This will take you to the selling page.

Step 3: Choose a Listing Format
Select the listing format that suits your product:

* **"Sell It Now":** Allows buyers to purchase immediately at a fixed price.
* **"Auction":** Buyers bid on your item, and the highest bidder wins.

Step 4: Provide Item Details
Fill in the item details:

* **Title:** Write a clear and concise title that describes your item accurately.
* **Category:** Choose the appropriate category and subcategory for your item.

Summarizing some of ChatGPT's features:

To date (2023), by utilizing ChatGPT 3.5 version, you can perform the following tasks for your branding and marketing needs, also known as Prompt Engineering:

1. Ask a specific or general question, and/or brainstorm.
2. Can get further details or answers, which may be creative or factual (depending on your requests), by using commands such as *List, Summarize, Compare, Expand, Give Pros and Cons, Pretend you are,* etc. Be very specific with your commands.
3. Ask for suggestions or ideas, and recommendations such as *"What type of influencers can I use to promote my sneaker brand?"*
4. Language translation for broader global outreach.
5. Comparative Analysis between markets, trends, and competitors.
6. Step-by-step instructions and research.

Disclaimer: *Please note that some information provided by ChatGPT may not be accurate as the data is being pulled from different sources on the Internet. Please make sure to Fact-Check information before using it, as well as rewrite or rephrase information that will be used in blogs, newsletters, etc., to avoid plagiarism.*

Tools & Resources
Building funnels - clickfunnels.com
ChatGPT – chat.openai.com
e-Commerce websites: Shopify, Wix, SquareSpace
Marketing Automation: https://zapier.com/

CHAPTER 11
THE POWER OF VIDEOS & LIVE STREAMING

These days creating a video to promote your brand is made easy with simple DIY platforms, programs and apps, that adequately allow video formation, built-in animation, image templates, and facilitate downloads. Live streaming is even more powerful at providing real time updates and offers on product launch.

Marketers create video content to drive traffic, increase awareness, sales, profits and even customer retention. In the last decade alone, videos have become the top 5% online marketing tool because they offer a stronger source of engagement. There are various types of videos such as promotional product videos, interviews about services and demo videos. Live streaming such as webinars and podcasts offer live footage and question and answer sessions about company offers. Important promotional video facts:

- They can be around 5 seconds to 2 minutes.
- Use action words, keep it simple and to the point. During and at the end of the video, there should be a very clear call to action, such as Subscribe Now, Buy Now, etc.
- More online customers engage in video content and therefore your videos should be viewed where customers are – on YouTube and social media.
- Videos can improve your company's or product's SEO ratings.
- Promo videos can be included on websites, blogs, in email marketing and on landing pages and funnels.
- You can include all your products or just your main product.
- In the video, don't forget to include your company's logo, name, email address and website link.

Many business owners struggle with what to say in their videos, or on a podcast. Creating content that is engaging can be challenging. However, as mentioned in the previous chapter, ChatGPT can be used to brainstorm ideas for short videos scripts to promote your brand on Instagram, Facebook Reels, and YouTube Shorts by customizing the command to suit your specific need. For example, you may need a casual video script idea for your online streetwear clothing store. Use ChatGPT to craft the blueprint (outline) for your script which you will later customize to suit your brand. Tweaking your script to be creative and engaging helps the narrative to resonate with the brand, as well as captivate your audience, thereby increasing content viewership. The more eyes on your content, the higher the probability of product sales and the greater the brand's market share.

Finally, online companies like Vimeo help businesses to increase customer engagement with interactive videos for video marketing and Live streaming.

Tools & Resources
Video marketing: be.live, canva.com, renderforest.com
Scripting ideas using ChatGPT: chat.openai.com
Interactive videos and Live streaming: https://vimeo.com/features/interactive-video

CHAPTER 12
BRANDING OFFLINE

Online branding doesn't mean that branding offline becomes obsolete. While you're selling online, you should also be visible offline. How is this done?

Here are 5 effective ways:

1. **Show up at trade shows, craft fairs, farmer's markets (whichever applies to your brand), armed with brochures, business cards, and of course your product.** While you're there to sell and promote, you also want to leave the consumer or the interested browser with something tangible. I find wearing the brand to be an effective conversation starter. Imagine standing talking to customers at a job fair while wearing a blazer with your recruiting company's logo embroidered on the collar or lapel, surrounded by professionally designed brochures, posters and even a banner. This suggests the company has a strong brand image. Even better, leave the customer with branded memorabilia, such as a key ring or a refrigerator magnet – they'll think of you every time they see it.

2. **Become a walking billboard for your brand.** Nothing says it quite as well as a graphic designed t-shirt with your logo and website address stamped on the front/back. Or if your brand is about sustainability, consider printing your logo and website on a cotton tote bag that you can always carry around with you.

3. **Volunteer.** Consider giving your time for events that are relatable to your brand. In this way, you are reaching more customers with whom your brand has a common interest. For example, if you're in the business of creating customized pet photography look-books, then consider volunteering at a dog show. While it's forbidden to solicit at most events like this (please make sure to follow the rules), it would be okay to donate free photography services at the event. By doing this, the event manager will ask for your networking materials such as brochures and business cards to make them available to the dog owners. If they like your photographs, chances are they'll contact you or visit your website to learn more about your other offers.

4. **Host a free event.** You/Your company can host an event. The purpose of the event is not to make sales. It should be either a fun event or an educational one. For instance, if you're a mentor and life coach, you can host an empowerment seminar to give people a sample experience of what you offer. Of course, your promotional materials should be on a table at the back of the room, near the exit, so members of the audience can later visit your website and book a one-on-one mentorship session with you.

5. **Brand your shipping materials.** Have you ever ordered a product online and the package (box, bag or jar) in which it came is so beautiful, it becomes an actual keepsake? Imagine receiving a box of chocolates and keeping the branded box long after the chocolates are gone! Again, this helps to keep your brand in the forefront of your customers' minds. The major

component here is to always be visible; so even if the customer is not online, your brand is still seen offline.

Tools & Resources

Printing services for physical promotional materials: Canva.com Vistaprint.com

What kind of marketing strategies will you use?

Remember, you can use a combination of online and offline strategies.

_____

_____

_____

_____

_____

_____

_____

_____

_____

_____

_____

_____

_____

_____

_____

_____

_____

CONCLUSION

In all that you do, don't forget your customers and users. After all, they are the sole reason for a brand's existence and purpose.

The shopping experience is important to the consumer. Keep in mind:

> ➢ Seek to create consistency in your branding on all fronts – that is, in the brand's impression, image, and personality.

> ➢ The brand is the "face" of the company, and its logo and tagline are the "soul".

> ➢ Let your brand speak volume – giving it an effective voice that can be heard over the millions of brands existing in cyberspace by marketing SMART.

> ➢ Utilize technologies and artificial intelligence (AI) that can aid in your brand's development, advancement, and growth within its industry.

Finally, for the consumer, "first impression lasts" and you only have a 20-second window to leave a lasting one!

References

Be Live. (2023). Stream with impact. https://be.live/

Bluehost. (2023). Bluehost Web Hosting. https://www.bluehost.com/

BrandCrowd. (December 16, 2022). Logo Design Trends 2023. Blog. https://www.brandcrowd.com/blog/logo-design-trends-2023/

Canva. (2023). Online Graphic Design Platform. https://www.canva.com/

Canva Logo Designs. (2023). What makes a good logo? 10 design tips to follow. Blog. https://www.canva.com/learn/what-makes-a-good-logo/

Clickfunnels. (2023). Meet Clickfunnels. Website. https://www.clickfunnels.com/

Conner, L. (2019). What is logo recognition? And the 5 best logo recognition tools. Blog | 99designs. https://99designs.com/blog/logo-branding/logo-recognition/

Constant-Content. (2023). Constant quality content – without the agency. https://www.constant-content.com/

Creately. (2023). The new interface for work. https://creately.com/

Edraw. (2023). Brand Resonance Pyramid Template. https://www.edrawsoft.com/template-brand-resonance-pyramid.html

Facebook. (2023). https://www.facebook.com/

Godaddy. (2022-2023). Building your website is very easy. https://www.godaddy.com/

Graphics & Charts. (2023). Canva. What will you design today? https://www.canva.com/

Hubspot. (2023). Software, Tools, Resources for Your Business. Grow Better with Hubspot. Hubspot Inc. https://www.hubspot.com/hp

Instagram. (2023). https://www.instagram.com/

Intuit Mailchimp. (2001-2023). Turn Emails into Revenue. https://mailchimp.com/

Legal Zoom. (2023). We're the one-stop-shop for all your business formation, tax, and trademark needs. https://www.legalzoom.com/business/

Linkedin. (2023). https://www.linkedin.com/

Namevine. (2023). Instantly find a Domain. https://namevine.com/

Oliver | Looka (June 6, 2023). The 10 Best Logo Redesigns of 2023 (So Far). Blog. https://looka.com/blog/logo-redesigns-2023/

Patel, Neil. (2023). Neil Patel. Website. https://neilpatel.com/

People Images/Getty Images. (2018, January 3). 9 Things to Do Differently If You're Working Out Regularly but Not Seeing the Workout Results You Want. Getty Image. https://www.self.com/story/things-to-do-differently-if-working-out-regularly-but-not-seeing-results

Pinterest. (2023). https://www.pinterest.com/

Rebelo, M. (August 1, 2023). The 11 best AI tools for social media management in 2023. Blog | Zapier Inc. https://zapier.com/blog/best-ai-social-media-management/

Renderforest. All your design tools in one place. https://www.renderforest.com/

Repustate. 2021. Understand How to Perform Logo Detection and Recognition in Videos. Blog | Repustate - Sprout Social. https://www.repustate.com/blog/logo-detection/#:~:text=How%20Is%20Logo%20Detection%20Done%20With%20Video%20AI%3F,in%20comments%20...%206%206.%20Visualize%20data%20

Shopify. (2023). Making Commerce Better for Everyone. https://www.shopify.com/

SquareSpace. (2023). Make any template yours with ease. https://www.squarespace.com/templates

SurveyMonkey. (2023). Free Online Survey Tool for Any Purpose. https://www.surveymonkey.com/

Tjibaria. (2020). FLC Workshop. https://tjibaria.clickfunnels.com/website35107342

Twitter. (2023). https://twitter.com/

Vimeo. (2023). Interactive Videos. https://vimeo.com/features/interactive-video

Vistaprint. (2023). Vistaprint. Website. https://www.vistaprint.com/

Wikipedia. (Updated August 19, 2023). Hero's journey. https://en.wikipedia.org/wiki/Hero%27s_journey

Wix. (2023). Free Website Builder and Business Solutions. Create a Website Without Limits. https://www.wix.com/

Xtensio. (2023). User Persona Template. https://xtensio.com/user-persona-template/

Zapier. (2023). Scale Success with Automation. https://zapier.com/

NOTES

NOTES

ABOUT THE AUTHOR

Dawnette Blackwood-Rhoomes MBA, is a Brand & Marketing Specialist and Coach for several online businesses, as well as Marketing Director for a non-profit providing educational services. She has 15+ years of experience in Graphic & Textile Design, Branding and Marketing. Dawnette is also a published author.

ISBN: 9798859658329